BIRDS

common kestrel

NATIONAL GEOGRAPHIC NATURE LIBRARY

BIRDS

NATIONAL GEOGRAPHIC NATURE LIBRARY

by K. M. Kostyal

NATIONAL GEOGRAPHIC SOCIETY

Washington, D.C.

*All photographs supplied by
Animals Animals/Earth Scenes*

scarlet macaw

blue-and-yellow macaw

Table of Contents

calliope hummingbird

osprey

WHAT IS A BIRD? 6

Our Feathered Friends 8

Hide and Seek 10

Those Amazing Flying Machines 12

On the Move 14

Nest Builders 16

1 Hunters of the Sky 18

Armed and Dangerous 20

The Clean-up Crew 22

2 Fowl Facts 24

3 Waders 26

A Shore Thing 28

4 Water Wonders 30

The Mating Game 32

Ocean Wanderers 34

Life at Sea 36

American avocet

blue-footed booby

5 Realm of the Flightless **38**
Penguin Power 40

6 Fancy Flightwork **42**
Fly Away Home 44

7 Climbers and Hole Nesters **46**
Agile Acrobats 48
Woodland Carpenters 50

8 Pretty Perchers **52**
Whistle a Happy Tune 54

Did You Know… 56
Glossary 58
Index 59   Credits 60

little blue penguin

*common
swift*

*purple
honeycreeper*

red-billed hornbill

WHAT IS A BIRD?

Just about every time you go outside, you probably see birds flying or hear them twittering around you. Birds live everywhere—on land, rivers, and lakes; at sea; and, of course, in the air. They come in all sizes, colors, and shapes. Some birds can't fly; others are great swimmers. Some are bigger than a man, and others are smaller than your thumb.

Birds may look very different from each other, but they are alike in these ways:

- They have WINGS.
- They are VERTEBRATES (VURT-uh-bruts).
- They BREATHE AIR.
- They hatch from SHELLED EGGS.
- They are WARM-BLOODED.
- They have BILLS BUT NO TEETH.
- They have FEATHERS AND WISHBONES.

tree swallow

greater flamingo

Cape petrel

red-faced cormorant

hoopoe

wood duck

6

golden eagle

eastern
meadowlark

carmine bee-eater

Steller's
jay

streamertail

burrowing
owl

brown kiwi

7

Our Feathered Friends

flight feather

Birds are the only animals that have feathers, and they have lots of them. Each bird has thousands of feathers that keep it warm and dry, help it fly, and help it attract a mate. Birds have different types of feathers, and each kind of feather has a specific use. One of the world's oldest birds, the feathered *Archaeopteryx* (ar-kee-OP-ter-ix), evolved from reptiles about 150 million years ago.

FEATHER FEATURES
Long flight feathers give a bird the lift and power to fly. Contour feathers give it shape and let air flow easily over its chest and back. Fuzzy down feathers next to a bird's skin keep it warm and dry.

contour feather

down feather

ANCIENT FLYER
A fossil of *Archaeopteryx* found in limestone in Germany clearly shows its feathers and its long, reptile-like tail. *Archaeopteryx* had claws on its fingertips, a feature left over from its reptile ancestors.

Some people call anhingas "snake birds" because of their long necks.

HANGING OUT TO DRY
An anhinga spreads its wings to dry in the sun. These birds are good divers and live around marshes and ponds. With their snake-like necks and wide wings, they look like ancient *Archaeopteryx*.

PROUD AS A PEACOCK ▶
Showing off for his lady friend, a peacock displays his elegant feathers. Many male birds have eye-catching feathers, called plumage, that help them attract females.

8

Hide and Seek

Like most animals, birds have natural camouflage that lets them blend in with their surroundings. You can often tell the kind of habitat a bird lives in by the color and pattern of its feathers. They usually match the color and pattern of the leaves, sand, grasses, or other parts of the bird's environment. Camouflage makes it hard for enemies to see a bird, especially if it keeps still.

Some birds, like the ptarmigan (TAR-mih-gen), change color with the seasons. In winter they're white, and in summer they are brown.

HIDING PLACE
Hiding beneath a blooming cactus, a horned lark chick is hard to spot. Its markings blend with the open grasslands where it lives, making it hard to see.

AS WHITE AS SNOW
In the cold flatlands of the Arctic, a snowy owl needs white plumage for camouflage so that its prey (PRAY) won't see it coming. A skillful hunter, this mighty owl feeds on small mammals.

LEAF PEEPER

Nestled among the dry leaves on a forest floor, a pauraque (por-OCK-ee) blends right in. Active at night, pauraques belong to a group of birds whose loud calls have earned them the name "nightjars."

LMOST INVISIBLE

he brown and black markings of merican woodcock chicks match e colors around their ground nest. eathers will replace their fluffy own as they get older, and the tterns and colors of the plumage ll be less fuzzy and more distinct.

11

Those Amazing Flying Machines

Champion fliers, birds take to the air with the greatest of ease. That's because their bodies are specially adapted for flying. Their muscles are powerful, especially the breast muscles that move their wings, and their skeletons are lightweight, strong, and compact. Most birds have hollow bones with air sacs in them. Their feathers act as little kites that let them ride the wind.

A parrot's broad wings and tail help it to maneuver.

WINGING IT

A bird's wings are adapted for the kind of flying it does. Gulls and other seabirds have long, slim wings to glide over the water. The wide, slotted wings of hawks and other birds of prey allow them to soar high. Plump-bodied birds such as quail have short, round wings to lift them off the ground quickly.

Hummingbirds can hover like helicopters, and they can even fly backward.

gull wing

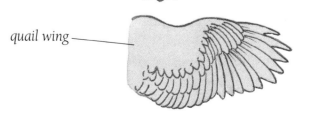

hawk wing

quail wing

BEAUTIFUL FLIERS

Hummingbirds, like this one—a calliope (kuh-LYE-uh-pea)— are amazing fliers. Their small wings move so fast in flight that they look like a blur and make a humming sound. In just one second, a calliope hummingbird beats its wings about 50 times.

IT'S A STRETCH

Wings extended, an Amazon parrot seeks a perch in the rain forest where it lives. The bones in birds' wings are somewhat like the bones in your arm, with a "forearm," a "wrist," and a "hand."

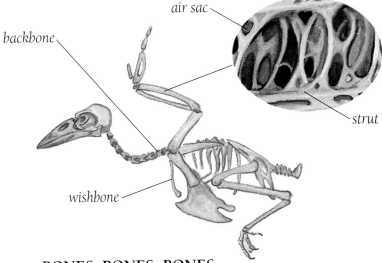

air sac

backbone

strut

wishbone

COMING
N FOR
A LANDING

As it gets close o its nest, a tree wallow puts on he brakes by urning its body perpendicular to he ground and spreading out its ail feathers.

BONES, BONES, BONES

A bird's backbone is an important part of a skeleton that supports many other bones. The bones of flying birds are light. They are hollow and filled with air. Inside each bone, other thin struts of bone strengthen the air-filled spaces.

13

On the Move

Huge flocks of birds wing through the sky in spring and fall. That's when many birds are on the move—migrating. They spend the spring and summer in one place. In the autumn, when the days get shorter and the weather cools, they fly off to someplace warmer, which may be thousands of miles away. Many birds return to the same summer nesting areas and winter grounds year after year. They seem to have a special sense of direction that acts like a compass and tells them which way to go. Migrating birds can fly for long stretches without stopping or eating.

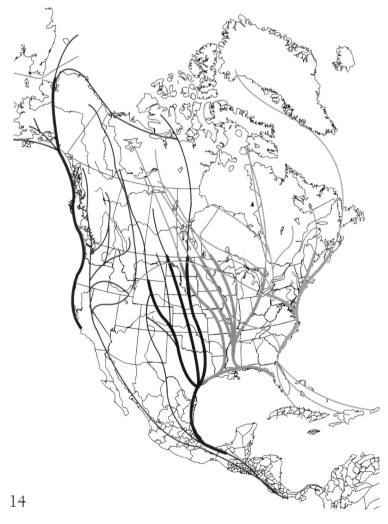

FLYWAY HIGHWAYS
In North America migrating geese, ducks, and swans usually follow certain routes when they travel south from their summer to their winter homes and return north again. Four major "bird highways," called flyways, stretch across the continent.

EESE GALORE

e sky turns white when snow geese
e on the move. Like most other wild
ese, snow geese fly north for the
mmer. They mate and nest in the
rctic grasslands of northern Canada,
aska, and Siberia. Snow geese fly as
r south as Mexico for the winter.

BLUE GOOSE

In summer a snow goose
sits on its nest in Arctic
grasslands. This snow
goose has blue feathers,
but most snow geese are
bright white.

15

Nest Builders

Every spring birds lay eggs and raise their young. First they must find a safe place and materials for a nest. Some birds hide their nests on the ground; many build in bushes or trees. Birds make nests of twigs, dry grass, leaves, mud, hair, feathers—even string.

WEED WEAVERS ▶
A female marsh wren uses the plants in marshes to bu[ild] a nest. She weaves the leav[es] of reeds, cattails, and bulrushes together to make the outer layer of the nest, then lines the inside with feathers and fine grasses.

ALL TUCKED IN
Safe in their straw-and-mud nest in the corner of a porch, barn swallow chicks wait to be fed. Their parents fly hundreds of miles a day to find insects for them to eat.

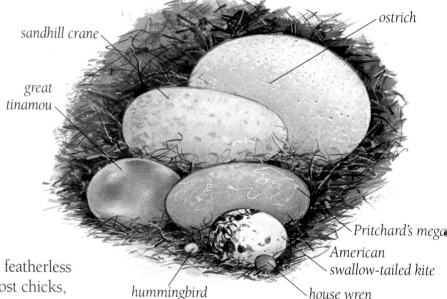

sandhill crane

great tinamou

ostrich

Pritchard's mega[pode]

American swallow-tailed kite

hummingbird

house wren

BALD BABES
A kingfisher's hatchlings are featherless and helpless at first. Like most chicks, they need a lot of care. The parent must bring them their meals.

Kingfishers lay several eggs before they start to incubate (IN-kyu-bate) them, or warm them so they will hatch. Some birds lay only one egg.

EGGS-TRAORDINARY
From blue to brown, from speckled to solid, from round to pointed, from big to little, birds' eggs come in all varieties. Sandhill crane eggs are almost four inches long, while those of the house wren are a little more than half an inch in length. Hummingbirds lay eggs less than half an inch long, the smallest of all birds. The ostrich lays the biggest egg of any living bird; an ostrich egg is almost seven inches long.

16

Hunters of the Sky

Eagles, hawks, falcons, ospreys, and owls are all amazing hunters, so they are called birds of prey. As they soar through the sky, they scan the area below for food. When they spot a mouse, a fish, a bird, or other small animal that would make a tasty meal, they dive at it like a missile and snatch it with sharp talons.

SKY KING
Ripping into its prey, a bald eagle chows down on a fish it caught. These mighty birds live around water and usually feed on fish, though they also hunt small mammals. Recently endangered, the bald eagle has made a strong comeback and once again lives all over North America.

Its fierce looks have made the bald eagle famous as the national bird of the United States.

The eagle's hooked beak makes a powerful tool to tear into prey, both dead and alive.

An osprey carries its fish dinner with the head facing forward. A sideways fish would slow its flight!

FISH ARE FAVORITES
Ospreys, also known as fish hawks, live near seacoasts, bays, large rivers, and lakes throughout the world.

EEKABOO
by barn owls look like balls of fluff with faces. Owls have flat, sh-shaped faces that direct sound to their ears and help them d prey at night, when they hunt. Owls use their ears to guide em to rodents, birds, and the other animals they eat.

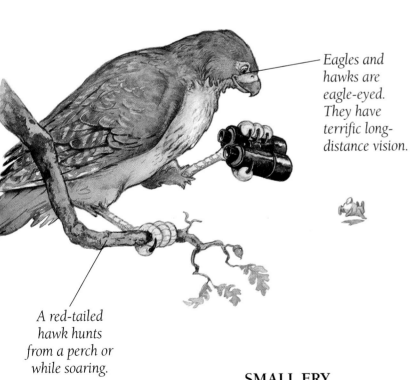

Eagles and hawks are eagle-eyed. They have terrific long-distance vision.

A red-tailed hawk hunts from a perch or while soaring.

The American kestrel's rust-colored back and striped face make it easy to identify.

SMALL FRY
A pint-size falcon, the American kestrel stands less than a foot high.

19

Armed and Dangerous

Birds of prey have some pretty powerful weapons. Their keen eyes let them spot their prey, even when it is far below. Equipped with long, sharp claws called talons (TA-luns), birds of prey can swoop down on a fish or other small animal and grab it, then keep a tight grip on it while they carry it off. Their hooked beaks are awesome tools that tear into captured prey and pull it apart.

A haw... brow b protect its eyes

KEEPING AN EYE OUT

Hawks have the hooked beaks and big, farsighted eyes that make birds of prey such skilled hunters.

FACE LIKE A DISH

Northern harriers live in marshes covered by thick grasses. To find prey hidden in the dense cover, harriers hunt by sound. Their faces, like those of owls, are dish-shaped and focus sounds to the birds' ears.

A harrier fans its tail to slow down and extends its legs to take prey.

DEADLY SILENCERS

The feathers of owls' wings have a special fringed edge. This makes their flight quieter so that they can sneak up on prey.

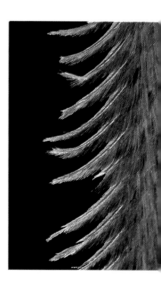

OWL EYES ▶

Small enough to squeeze into a hole a woodpecker made in a cactus, the elf ov is a good hunter. An owl's eyes face straight ahead. To see things to the side or behind, it must turn its head.

Curved talons help control prey.

GREAT GRIPPERS

Strong talons give birds of prey a great grip, but they're not so good for walking. You won't see these birds out for a stroll, the way you might a quail or a robin.

20

The Clean-up Crew

If you see big, dark birds circling together in the sky, they are probably vultures. Vultures feed on carrion (CARE-ee-un)—dead animals. That may not sound very appetizing, but vultures play an important role. They help keep the landscape clean.

SHARING A ROOST
When it's time to rest, turkey vultures gather together at a favorite roosting pla These birds often roost together for safet They may spread their wings out as they rest to catch the warmth of the sun.

LUNCH BUNCH
African vultures like to eat leftovers. When a large hunter, such as a lion, has killed an animal and eaten its fill, vultures move in to tear at the remains. Because vultures feed on dead animals they find, they are called scavengers (SKAV-en-jers).

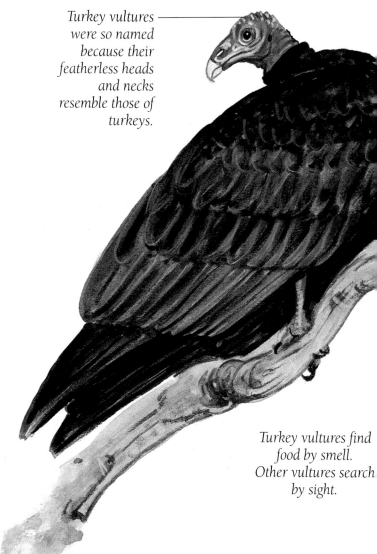

Turkey vultures were so named because their featherless heads and necks resemble those of turkeys.

Turkey vultures find food by smell. Other vultures search by sight.

The wingspan of a turkey vulture measures six feet .

The thick, fleshy growth across a vulture's beak is called a caruncle (CAR-un-kul).

BALD IS BEAUTIFUL
Like other members of the vulture family, the king vulture of Mexico and South America has a bald head and neck. A bald head is easier to keep clean while eating messy food. The bare skin of its head and upper neck is orange, red, and blue.

2 Fowl Facts

All the plump-bodied birds that are shaped much like a chicken are called fowl. There are hundreds of different kinds and sizes of fowl living all over the world, except in Antarctica and some remote islands. The males often have eye-catching plumage. Most fowl eat grain, berries, seeds, and buds. They feed their young on insects. Because people sometimes hunt them, wild fowl are called game birds.

WHAT A DANDY
Trying to impress females, a male greater prairie-chicken inflates orange air sacs on each side of its neck. Some male birds even dance to attract mates.

CRESTED CUTIES
During fall and winter, California quails of the western U.S. often congregate together in groups called coveys (CUH-vees). While the rest of the covey pecks about on the ground for food, one quail may stand guard to watch for foxes and other predators, or hunters. In the spring the coveys break up as the quails pair into couples and begin to nest.

A tuft of feathers jutting from a bird's head is called a crest.

Male and female California quails have similar plumage. Only the male has black-and-white markings on its head and neck.

TAILS UP
A male sage grouse shows off to attract a female. It sticks its fanned tail high in the air and inflates its neck sacs. At mating time, several males strut in an area called a lek, then the females pick partners.

A male golden pheasant sports a cascade of feathers down its neck.

Pheasants have such beautiful plumage that people have carried them from Asia to other continents for decoration.

GOLDIE LOCKS
Like most pheasants, the golden pheasant was originally from Asia, but now it is found in other parts of the world.

Relatives of golden pheasants roam fields and open woodlands in North America and Europe.

Chickens in farmyards like to establish a pecking order. The bossiest hen gets the best food and never gets pecked on, but all the chickens beneath her do.

Everybody picks on the weakest little chicken at the end of the line, and it gets less to eat.

③ Waders

Wading birds include long-legged lovelies such as herons, egrets, ibises, and cranes as well as short-legged shorebirds such as sanderlings. In addition to long legs, herons have long necks and bills that allow them to feed in deep water. They look down for prey, then thrust their bills underwater and make a quick grab for a fish, frog, crab, or insect.

Once they choose a mate, cranes stay together for life.

Like all cranes, African crowned cranes perform an elaborate courtship dance before they breed.

WHO NEEDS A FORK?
It's easy to see how the spoonbill got its name. When it's hungry, it sweeps its flat, spoon-shaped bill from side to side in the water. The sensitive bill feels small creatures and snaps them up. This Eurasian spoonbill winters in Africa and southern Asia.

TAKING OFF ▶
Winging its way up, a great egret begins its slow, graceful flight. These birds often nest together in big colonies. During the breeding season, great egrets grow long filmy feathers on their backs. Hunters killed thousands of these and other egrets for their plumes earlier in this century. Now plume hunting is illegal.

A Shore Thing

Many small waders, called shorebirds, live along coasts. When they are finished breeding, shorebirds gather in large flocks to feed and migrate. Some travel thousands of miles between nesting and wintering grounds.

Avocets have slender, turned-up bills. They swish the bills from side to side in water to capture insects and small shellfish at the surface.

BEACH BOYS

In winter, flocks of sanderlings skitter along the edge of the surf on ocean beaches. They wait for waves to come crashing in. Then, when the water recedes, they search the wet beach for sand fleas uncovered by the waves.

BACKWARD BEND!

Preparing to eat, an American avocet will bend its legs backward to reach the water with its long bill.

FINE FAKE

Like many small wading birds, killdeers nest on the ground. If they see an enemy coming near their eggs, they pretend to be hurt and run away from the nest dragging one wing. Usually the enemy follows the birds. Their name comes from their noisy *kill-DEE* call.

LADE BILLS

anding on mud flats, American ystercatchers probe the wet sand nd mud with their beaks, feeling r clams, crabs, and oysters. Once e birds find a shellfish, they ammer or pry open its shell with eir long, flat beaks and gobble up e soft animal inside.

Oystercatchers have large, red-orange bills.

WALKING ON WATER

With their big, spidery feet, purple gallinules can walk across floating plants without sinking. From the southern United States to South America, the bright colors of these birds can be spotted around ponds and marshes.

Water Wonders

ater birds have bodies built for swimming. Their webbed feet pull them forward in the water, the way your hands do when you swim. Water birds have very dense plumage and a thick layer of down feathers that help them keep warm in the water. Some dive far underwater in the ponds, lakes, rivers, and oceans where they live.

SUPER SLICKER

Oil on this whistling duck's feathers makes water roll off and keep its down feathers and skin dry. Birds use oil when they preen, or groom, their feathers. With their bills, they take the oil from a gland above their tails and rub it onto each feather.

Birds often put their heads on their backs when they rest or sleep. This helps the birds keep warm.

UPSIDE-DOWN DINNER

A mute swan thrusts its long neck underwater, tips its tail up, and paddles with its feet to reach water plants. A bird's reaching with its bill for food underwater is called dabbling.

HOVERCRAFT

To find food, Wilson's storm-petrels hover so close to the ocean that their feet dangle in the water. Millions of them gather to breed in the cold lands in and around Antarctica.

GANGWAY FOR GOSLINGS

Compared to most birds, Canada goose families stay together a long time. When they learn to fly, most young birds leave their parents. But goose chicks, called goslings, stay with their parents for a year and learn the migration route they use.

31

The Mating Game

Some water birds spend winters on the seacoast, then migrate to inland ponds and lakes for the warm months. In these protected places, they nest, lay eggs, and raise their young. Before they do those things, most birds go through a courtship ritual. For western grebes and other water birds, courtship can be a long, elaborate dance.

Bashful boy, this male grebe has his neck curved downward as he brings his lady a weedy present.

FLIRTING ALONG
If a male and female western grebe decide they like each other, they may sink their bodies low in the water and float along together. This is called barging, because they bump along like barges.

DANCES WITH WEEDS
When courting, western grebes waggle weeds at each other. This is called a weed dance, and it means "You're the one for me."

GETTING THE RUSH!
Running across the water, western grebes keep their courtship moving by "rushing." After running a little way, they'll suddenly dive below the surface. Grebes zoom far underwater, even when they're not mating. Usually, they're looking for food or escaping from an enemy.

FAMILY AFFAIR

After the courtship is over, the grebes build
a nest in tall reeds near—or even floating on—
the water, then lay their eggs. The parents take
turns sitting on the eggs. After about three weeks,
the eggs hatch, and out come tiny gray grebe
chicks. When the chicks are young, their parents
often carry them piggyback across the water.

Ocean Wanderers

Seabirds can do some amazing things. They may migrate vast distances every year, and some wander the oceans for months at a time without ever setting down on land. Some have huge wingspans that let them soar effortlessly across the seas. The two species of great albatross—the wandering and the royal—which circle the waters around Antarctica, have the longest wingspans of any birds in the world! Some seabirds sport awesomely colored bills, or feet, or throat sacs.

TO THE ENDS OF THE EARTH

Each year arctic terns travel from the top of the world to the bottom—and back. These medium-size birds spend their summers in the waters near the Arctic Circle. In the fall they fly south—and south and south—all the way to Antarctica, a distance of 10,000 miles. That's a round-trip journey of 20,000 miles a year!

WIDE-WINGED WANDERERS

Wandering albatrosses glide on stiff, outstretched wings over the southern oceans of the world looking for squid. Skimming low over the waves, the birds often follow ships and fishing boats for hours, waiting for scraps of food the crews may throw overboard.

FABULOUS FEET

Blue-footed boobies don't have cold feet, in spite of their color. In fact, the blue color absorbs heat. When boobies incubate their eggs, their feet act like heating pads. Boobies are great divers. Starting high in the air, they plunge straight into the water, grabbing fish with their sharp bills.

Boobies display their colorful feet during a courtship dance.

The average wingspan of a wandering albatross measures more than ten feet.

SHOW-OFF

A male frigatebird has a sac on its neck that it blows up like a big red balloon to attract females. Frigatebirds soar high above the sea on narrow wings. They are pirates, chasing boobies and other seabirds and stealing their food.

35

Life at Sea

Seabirds often nest in rocky cliffs facing the ocean. Because nesting space like that is hard to find, different species of birds will nest in the same cliffs. Each species forms its own colony and fights hard to keep other birds out. And seabirds have the sharp bills to do it. Crooked, straight, wide, narrow, yellow, black, red, and blue—the bills of seabirds vary in shape and color. Most seabirds use their bills for fishing. Some spear fish; others grab prey from the water or scoop it up with their beaks.

To break open the shells of clams and oysters, gulls drop the shellfish from high in the air onto rocks.

Then they have to race down and claim their meal before another hungry gull grabs it.

FEATHERING THEIR NEST
Atlantic puffins line their nests in hillside burrows with mouthfuls of feathers that keep the nests soft and warm. During spring courtship, brightly colored horny plates cover a puffin's bill. In late summer puffins head out to sea, and the elaborate bill coverings fall off, leaving their beaks smaller and gray for the winter.

Wings folded back, dive-bombing pelicans crash straight into the water. for fish.

Air sacs under a pelican's skin cushion its dive and make it pop back up to the surface after it hits.

Its bill opens wide, and its throat pouch forms a fishnet underwater.

BATH TIME

A brown pelican tosses water over its back. After bathing, it will preen its feathers back into place. Seabirds enjoy wet baths; some land birds clean themselves by dusting in sand.

KEEPING AN EYE OUT

Resting its head on its back, a brown pelican takes a little time out. Pelicans and other seabirds often grab a nap between feedings. They find a cozy spot on a beach and sit on the sand while they rest. At night, birds often roost, or sleep, in groups.

5 Realm of the Flightless

All birds have wings, but not all can fly. The enormous ostrich and its South American cousin, the rhea, are too big to get off the ground. Millions of years ago, they would have felt right at home, because a lot of huge, flightless birds walked the earth. Cassowaries, emus, and kiwis still roam Australia and New Zealand, and a few kinds of flightless ducks and parrots are scattered across the globe. Of course, everyone knows that penguins are flightless, too, but they make up for it by "flying" through the water.

Record runners, African ostriches can sprint at 40 miles an hour on their two-toed feet. That makes them not only the biggest birds in the world, but also the fastest on land.

FLEET FEET

The cassowary can't fly, but with oversize feet, it can run fast. If threatened by a human or other animal, it fights viciously, slashing out with strong, sharp claws.

BIG BIRD

The biggest birds on earth, African ostriches are taller than a man and weigh around 250 pounds. A bird that weighs over 40 pounds can't lift itself into the air, so flying is out for ostriches. Their small wings would never lift their heavy bodies, and their fluffy feathers would be no help in flight.

moa

dodo

great auk

GONE BUT NOT FORGOTTEN

A 50-pound pigeon called the dodo once lived on the Indian Ocean island of Mauritius. Moas up to 13 feet tall wandered through New Zealand, and the penguin-like great auk fished the North Atlantic.

39

Penguin Power

Little birds in tuxedos—that's all most people think of penguins. But penguins are pretty amazing creatures. They live only in the Southern Hemisphere. On land, these flightless birds waddle around, but when they swim through the ocean, they become graceful fliers. Their paddle-like wings act like propellers, while their feet and tails serve as rudders. Some penguins can dive down 800 feet!

A penguin's wings are stiff and short. They don't fold across its back as the wings of most other birds do.

FURRY FELLOW
This little blue penguin's body feathers look almost like fur, but they are waterproof and keep out the cold.

POP GOES THE PENGUIN
When an enemy such as a leopard seal gets too close, swimming Adélie penguins jump straight out of the water and onto a nearby chunk of ice to escape danger.

A penguin's wings help it balance on land.

CALL THEM MACARONI
Just like Yankee Doodle, who "put a feather in his cap and called it macaroni," these macaroni penguins have crests of gold feathers. They belong to a group called crested penguins.

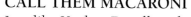

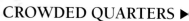

CROWDED QUARTERS ▶
Along the steep and rocky coasts of the Southern Hemisphere, there aren't many places where penguins can land. So, they crowd onto any patch they can reach. During the nesting season, the shoreline may be covered with a colony of thousands of the birds.

6 Fancy Flightwork

Birds are real athletes of the air. Some can fly for a long time without stopping; others fly incredibly fast. The world's fastest bird is probably the peregrine falcon. In a dive after prey, it may reach speeds of more than a hundred miles per hour. The eider, a type of duck, has been clocked in steady, horizontal flight going nearly 50 miles per hour.

STUNT FLIER

Hummingbirds are fast and acrobatic. They have pointed wings that sweep back at their sides like those of high-speed planes. When a hummingbird hovers, it rotates its wings at the shoulder so that they turn completely over going backward as well as forward. Most birds get power for flight from the "hand" part at the tip of their wings and lift from the feathers of the "forearm."

THAT'S SWIFT

An ace flier, the swift zooms through the air on long, tapered wings. As it flies, it beats its wings quickly, glides a little, then beats its wings again. Most, if not all, swifts roost at night in caves, hollow trees, folded leaves, or chimneys.

A hummingbird's wingtips make a figure-eight pattern as it hovers.

The feet and legs of a hummer, such as this rubythroat, are tiny.

With a beak like a straw, a hummer can suck nectar out of a flower while hovering.

As they fly, nighthawks ?le up moths and other ?nsects. Long ?ristles at the ?ides of their mouths help ?em net prey.

A broad, stiff tail acts like a rudder to help the hummer steer while flying.

MIGHTY MITE
Hummingbirds are the tiniest members of the bird world. Rufous hummers live in western North America.

Fly Away Home

In almost any city park, you can see pigeons strutting around. Strong fliers, pigeons are adaptable birds and live in most places. Some people keep pigeons as pets and train them. If you let these birds loose far from home, they can still find their way back. More than 150 years ago, billions of wild pigeons called passenger pigeons lived in America. The skies turned black as huge flocks of them flew overhead. These pigeons were hunted to extinction. The last one died in the Cincinnati Zoo in 1914.

BILLING AND COOING
When a male and female pigeon are courting, they make cooing sounds and nibble each other's necks with their bills. Pigeon parents produce a milk-like liquid in their throats that they feed to their chicks.

SITTING PRETTY
A female pigeon builds the nest, using twigs brought to her by the male bird. Pigeons and doves eat mostly grain, other seeds, and fruit.

Most pigeons and doves build flimsy nests of sticks.

Among the fastest fliers in the bird world, homing pigeons carried messages during wartime before reliable portable radios became available.

GRABBING A DRINK

Pigeons, which survive well in cities, are descended from wild rock doves that were brought to this country from Europe almost 400 years ago. Rock doves nest in cliffs. That's why city pigeons nest on the ledges of tall buildings.

7

Climbers and Hole Nesters

Birds can be good climbers as well as fliers. Climbing birds have strong legs and can hold tight to tree trunks. Some use their tails to help support themselves while they climb. Others use their bills to pull themselves upward. Many climbing birds build nests in holes. They might peck out a place in a tree trunk or dig a burrow.

TREE HOUSE

Like other hornbills, the great hornbill of Asia makes sure its nest is safe by sealing it shut. Once the female lays her eggs in a tree hole, the male plasters her in with mud. He leaves a slit so that he can pass food in for her and the chicks.

ANYBODY HOME?

With its long, colorful beak, an African red-billed hornbill digs out a nesting hole. Inside, his mate will lay her eggs.

Kingfishers loosen the dirt with their long bills, then push it out with their feet.

HOME SWEET HOME

Kingfishers often nest in tunnels they dig in the banks of rivers and streams. The birds dig tunnels up to seven feet long.

REACH FOR IT ▶

Related to woodpeckers, toucans nest in the holes of tall trees in the American tropics. With their long but light beaks, toucans can reach fruits or berries on the very tip of a branch.

Agile Acrobats

In the forests and grasslands of the world, there are hundreds of kinds of wild parrots flying free. They use their claws and beaks almost like hands, climbing trees with them or hanging upside down from limbs. Parrots often live together in chattering, screeching flocks. Once big flocks of Carolina parakeets fluttered through forests in the southern and eastern United States. Now they are extinct.

A hooked bill helps parrots crack open and eat nuts and seeds.

FIG FEAST
A fig parrot's meal is the same color as it is. A little bird of the South American rain forest, the fig parrot scrapes the meat out of figs with its curved bill. It also uses its bill as a shovel, digging nests in tree limbs and trunks.

RAINBOW BIRDS
Real sweet eaters, rainbow lorikeets of Australia feed on pollen and nectar from flowers. They'll even eat the flowers themselves! Lorikeets and parakeets are small members of the parrot family.

HANGING IN THERE
Plum-headed parakeets use claws and beaks to dangle from trees in the woodlands and forests of southeastern Asia.

Parakeets use their strong beaks to grab seeds, berries, and other fruits.

49

Woodland Carpenters

The sound of something tapping on a tree usually means that a woodpecker is at work. Woodpeckers use their bills as chisels to make nesting holes in trees or to find food. They listen for insects moving under a tree's bark, then they chop out a little hole in the trunk and probe or spear insects with their long, barbed tongues.

PECKING PARTNERS

A group of acorn woodpeckers often hammer at the same tree together, making a neat line of holes around its bark. They tuck acorns away in the holes, saving them for the winter months when food is hard to find.

HAMMER HEAD

Hard at work, a red-headed woodpecker hacks into the soft wood of a dead tree. It's probably starting to chip out a nesting hole. Super strong neck muscles give the bird its hammering power.

Woodpeckers use their strong, pointed tail feathers as props to brace themselves against trees.

DINNERTIME

A young flicker sticks its bill out of the nest, ready for some grub. Like almost all woodpeckers, flickers have strong claws, with two toes pointing forward and two backward. A flicker's stiff tail helps support its weight when it's climbing.

Large woodpeckers, flickers have dark markings across their backs. In eastern North America these birds have yellow underwings and tails; those in the west have red.

WOODY WOODPECKER

The crow-size pileated woodpecker pounds deep into trees to get beetle larvae and ants. To cushion its brain during all that hammering, a woodpecker has a thick skull.

Bristly feathers in a woodpecker's nostrils keep out flying wood chips.

51

8

Pretty Perchers

The kind of bird you probably see most often near your home is a perching bird. Swallows, thrushes, wrens, warblers, and even crows perch on tree limbs or fence posts. The most successful of birds, perchers live all over the world, and there are more of them than any other group of birds. Because most perching birds are such good singers, people also call them songbirds.

tail plume

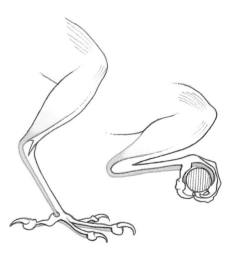

UPSIDE-DOWN PERCHER
A male blue bird of paradise goes all out to attract females. He hangs upside down and fans out his feathers, exposing a reddish black patch on his breast. Two long tail plumes bend almost double.

Honeycreepers also use their sharp bills to poke holes in the bases of flowers and suck out the nectar.

PRETTY IN PURPLE
To feed, purple honeycreepers perch on branches. They use their long, curved bills to reach into flowers for nectar and to grab insects.

GETTING A GRIP
The tendons in a songbird's feet automatically grasp tightly when the bird perches.

COOL CHARACTER

The black-capped chickadee is a pretty tough character when it comes to cold. By fluffing up its feathers, it can trap warm air around its body and survive winter weather just fine. Eating a lot of energy-rich food, such as seeds, also helps small songbirds stay warm. That's why they often cluster at bird feeders.

PARKED ON A PERCH

Comfortable on a strand of barbed wire, a yellow-rumped warbler looks almost footless. Its claws are holding on tight. Warblers migrate together in flocks of thousands, traveling only at night, navigating by the stars.

This warbler has yellow patches on its rump, crown, and sides.

Whistle a Happy Tune

When spring comes and it's time for nesting, songbirds fill the air with their music. Male birds usually do the singing to let females know they're available as mates. The males may also be claiming a certain territory as their own. If other male birds come into their area, the owners will chase them away. Each species of bird has a special song. So, all male robins whistle more or less the same tune. A bird may sing its song more than 1,500 times in a day. Scientists think that sometimes birds sing just for the joy of it.

HEAVENLY CROONER ▶
Head back, a male rose-breasted grosbeak belts out its long, sweet song. When two male grosbeaks are fighting over the same female, they both may hang around her and sing their hearts out.

SINGING FOR THEIR SUPPER
Mockingbird chicks try out their voices by squealing for food. Great singers, mockingbirds get their name from their ability to copy, or mock, other birds' songs. These chicks have feathers just sprouting from the skin on their wings.

Mockingbirds are such good mimics that they can even imitate a tinkling piano, a creaking wheelbarrow, or a house alarm.

54

The bird's voice box, or syrinx (SEAR-inks), is located in the lower part of its windpipe, where it branches to go to the lungs. Only birds have a syrinx.

Different kinds of songbirds prefer different perches for singing. This yellow-headed blackbird likes a cattail seat.

55

Did You Know...

1 **THAT** dippers can walk underwater. This American dipper, a kind of songbird, dives into fast-flowing streams high in the mountains of the West and looks for worms, water bugs, and shellfish to eat.

2 **THAT** the oxpecker is the friend of such African mammals as zebras, rhinoceroses, and buffalo. Munching on the ticks and other insects that bother these big guys, the oxpecker rides along with them and gets rid of their pests.

3 **THAT** the brush turkey incubates its eggs by heaping a huge mound of leaves and sand over them. As the vegetation decays, it gives off heat. The parent birds can tell whether the nest is warm enough or too warm for the eggs; they pile on more plants or take some off to keep the eggs at the right temperature.

4 **THAT** a black skimmer can glide right along the surface of water and snatch fish with its amazing bill. Only skimmers have bills whose lower half is much longer than the upper one. The longer lower half slices through the water. When it hits a fish, the skimmer closes the upper half of its bill to clamp down on the prey.

5 **THAT** hoatzin (waht-SEEN) chicks have large claws on their wings. They use their claws to climb through tree branches in the swamps of South America. As hoatzins grow older, they lose their claws, but they still use their wings to help in climbing.

6 **THAT** the saying "skinny as a rail" refers to a kind of bird. There are many different rails, and almost all of them live in marshes. A rail's skinny body allows it to squeeze through narrow gaps in reeds, cattails, and grasses.

Glossary

BREED To produce young.

CAMOUFLAGE A natural disguise, such as the color or pattern of feathers, that helps an animal blend with its surroundings.

CARRION Dead and rotting animals.

COLONY A group of birds living and nesting together.

COURTSHIP The behavior male and female birds go through prior to mating and nesting.

COVEY A small flock of game birds.

CREST Feathers on the top of a bird's head that can be raised.

DABBLE To use the bill to search for food in mud or shallow water, as swans, geese, and ducks do.

ENDANGERED In danger of becoming extinct.

EXTINCT No longer existing on earth.

HABITAT An animal's natural home, such as a forest, a desert, a river, or an ocean.

INCUBATE To warm eggs so that they will hatch.

MIGRATE To move from one area to another, usually in the spring or fall.

PLUMAGE A bird's feathers.

PREDATOR An animal that hunts and kills other animals for food.

PREENING A bird's cleaning, oiling, and arranging of its feathers.

PREY An animal that is hunted by other animals for food.

ROOST To rest or sleep, either alone or in groups.

SCAVENGER An animal that does not capture its own prey, eating instead dead animals left by other predators.

SPECIES A group of animals of the same kind that can produce young like themselves.

SYRINX A bird's voice box, located where its windpipe splits and goes to its two lungs.

TERRITORY An area claimed and defended by an animal or a group of animals.

VERTEBRATE An animal—fish, amphibian, reptile, bird, or mammal—with a backbone.

WARM-BLOODED Able to keep a constant body temperature even when the temperature of the surrounding varies.

WINGSPAN The measurement of an animal's outstretched wings from tip to tip.

dface indicates illustrations.

atrosses: royal 34; wandering
4-35
ninga 8
haeopteryx 8
, great 39
cet, American 4, 28

d of Paradise, blue 52
ds: bathing 37; bones 13;
amouflage 10-11;
haracteristics 6; eggs 16; feather
ypes 8, 20; flight adaptations
2-13, 42-43; migration 14, 15,
2, 34; nesting 16, 17, 28, 32-
3, 36, 44, 46; preening 30, 37;
osting 22-23; sleeping 37;
rinx 55; wings 12-13
ds of prey 18-21
kbird, yellow-headed 55
by, blue-footed 4, 35

ssowary 38
ckadee, black-capped 53
ickens: pecking order 24
mbing birds 48-49
nes 26; crowned 26
ws 52

pper, American 56
do 39
ves 44; rock 45
cks 14, 38; eider 42; whistling
0; wood 6

gles 18; bald 18; golden 7
ets 26; great 26, 27

Extinct birds 8, 39
Falcons 18, 19; peregrine 42
Flicker 51
Flightless birds 38-39
Flyways, North American
    (migration routes) 14
Fowl 24-25
Frigatebird 35

Gallinule, purple 29
Game birds 24-25
Geese: Canada 31; snow 14-15
Grebe, western 32-33
Grosbeak, rose-breasted 54, 55
Grouse, sage 24
Gulls 12, 36

Harrier, northern 20
Hawks 18, 20; red-tailed 19
Heron 26
Hoatzin 57
Honeycreeper, purple 5, 52
Hornbills: great 46; red-billed 5,
    46
Hummingbirds: calliope 4, 12;
    flight 42-43; rufous 43;
    streamertail 7

Ibis 26

Kestrels: American 19; common 1
Killdeer 28
Kingfishers 16, 46

Lark, horned 10
Lorikeet, rainbow 48

Macaws: blue-and-yellow 2-3;
    scarlet 2-3

Moa 39
Mockingbird 54

Nighthawk 43
Nightjar 11

Osprey 4, 18, 19
Ostrich, African 38, 39
Owls 18-21; barn 19; elf 20, 21;
    snowy 10
Oxpecker 56
Oystercatcher, American 29

Parakeets: Carolina 48; plum-
    headed 49
Parrots 48; Amazon 12-13; fig 48;
    flightless 38
Pauraque 11
Peacock 8, 9
Pelican, brown 37
Penguins 38, 40-41; Adélie 40;
    little blue 5, 40; macaroni 40
Perching birds 52-53
Pheasant 25; golden 25; ring-
    necked 25
Pigeons 44-45; homing 44;
    passenger 44
Prairie-chicken, greater 24
Ptarmigan 10
Puffin, Atlantic 36

Quail 12; California 24
Quetzal, resplendent 60

Rail 57
Rhea 38

Sanderlings 28
Scavengers 22-23

Seabirds 34-37
Skimmer, black 57
Snake bird see Anhinga
Songbirds 52-55
Spoonbill, Eurasian 26
Storm-petrel, Wilson's 31
Swallows 52; barn 16; tree 6, 13
Swans 14; mute 30
Swift, common 5, 42

Tern, arctic 34
Thrush 52
Toucan 46, 47
Turkey, brush 56

Vultures 22-23; African 22; king
    23; turkey 22-23

Wading birds 26-29
Warblers 52; yellow-rumped 53
Water birds 30-33
Woodcock, American 11
Woodpeckers 50-51; acorn 50;
    pileated 51; red-headed 50
Wrens 52; marsh 16, 17

Credits

resplendent quetzal

Published by
The National Geographic Society
Reg Murphy, *President
and Chief Executive Officer*
Gilbert M. Grosvenor,
Chairman of the Board
Nina D. Hoffman,
Senior Vice President
William R. Gray, *Vice President and Director
Book Division*

Staff for this Book
Barbara Lalicki, *Director of Children's Publishing*
Barbara Brownell, *Senior Editor and Project Manager*
Marianne R. Koszorus, *Senior Art Director and
Project Manager*
Toni Eugene, *Editor*
Alexandra Littlehales, *Art Director*
Sally Collins, *Illustrations Editor*
Amy Donovan, *Researcher*
Meredith Wilcox, *Illustrations Assistant*
Dale-Marie Herring, *Administrative Assistant*
Susan Fels, *Indexer*
Mark A. Caraluzzi, *Marketing Manager*
Vincent P. Ryan, *Manufacturing Manager*

Acknowledgments
We are grateful for the assistance of Dr. George E. Watson,
Committee for Research & Exploration, National Geographic
Society, *Scientific Consultant*. We also thank John Agnone and
Rebecca Lescaze, National Geographic Book Division, for their
guidance and suggestions.

Illustrations Credits

Front Cover: Frans Lanting/MINDEN PICTURES

Interior photographs from Animals Animals/Earth Scenes
Front Matter: 1 Stephen Dalton. 2-3 Mickey Gibson. 4 (top to bottom), Alan G. Nelson; Peter
Weimann; Wilfried D. Schurig; Patti Murray. 5 (top to bottom), John Eastcott & Yva Momatiuk;
Stephen Dalton; Ken Cole; Arthur Gloor. 6-7 (art), Warren Cutler. 8 (upper), Breck P. Kent; 8 (art
upper), Warren Cutler. 8 (lower), Stan Osolinski/OSF. 9 M. Austerman. 10 (art), Robert Cremins.
(left), Charles Palek. 10 (right), E.R. Degginger. 11 (upper), Michael Fogden. 11 (lower), Leonard L
Rue, III. 12 Alan G. Nelson. 12 (art), Robert Cremins. 12-13 Stephen Dalton. 13 (art), Warren Cutl
13 Joe McDonald. 14 (art), Robert Cremins. 15 Ken Cole. 14-15 Francis Lepine. 16 (art), Robert
Cremins. 16 (upper), Patti Murray. 16 (lower), Terry Heathcote/OSF. 17 Wilfried D. Schurig.
Birds of Prey: 18 Lynn M. Stone. 19 (art), Robert Cremins. 19 (right), Peter Weimann. 19 (left),
Willard Luce. 19 (lower), Joe McDonald. 20 (art, upper), Robert Cremins. 20 (art, lower), Warren
Cutler. 20 (left), R.H. Armstrong. 20 (right), G.I. Bernard/OSF. 21 Paul & Shirley Berquist. 22. Joe
McDonald. 22-23 (art), Warren Cutler. 23 Maresa Pryor.
Fowl: 24 (upper), Don Enger. 24 (left), Joe McDonald. 24 (right), Harry Engles. 25 (art), Robert
Cremins. 25 Maresa Pryor.
Wading Birds: 26 (art), Robert Cremins. 26 Robert Maier. 27 Henry Ausloos. 28 (left), Wilfried D.
Schurig. 28 (right & lower), John Trott. 29 (art) Warren Cutler. 29 Joe & Carol McDonald.
Water Birds: 30 (art), Warren Cutler. 30 David J. Boyle. 31 (art), Warren Cutler. 30-31 Gary W.
Griffen. 32 (art), Robert Cremins. 32-33 (all), Don Enger. 34 Robert Maier. 34-35 (art), Warren Cu
35 (upper), Patti Murray. 35 (lower), Richard Kolar. 36 (art), Robert Cremins. 36 Robert Maier. 37
(art), Robert Cremins. 37 (upper), Zig Leszczynski. 37 (lower), Ted Levin.
Flightless Birds: 38 (art), Robert Cremins. 38 Breck P. Kent. 39 (art), Warren Cutler. 39 Arthur G
40 (art), Robert Cremins. 40 (upper), John Eastcott & Yva Momatiuk. 40 (lower), Johnny Johnson.
A. Bannister.
Birds in Flight: 42 Stephen Dalton. (42-43) (art), Warren Cutler. 43 (art), Robert Cremins. 43 R.H
Armstrong. 44 (art), Robert Cremins. 44 (upper), Fritz Prenzel. 44 (lower), Hans & Judy Beste. 45 (
Bernard/OSF.
Climbers and Hole Nesters: 46 (art), Robert Cremins. 46 (left), Arthur Gloor. 46 (right) & 47
Stephen Dalton. 48 (left), Fritz Prenzel; 48 (right), Hans and Judy Beste; 49 (art), Warren Cutler. 50
(art), Robert Cremins. 50 Richard Day/Daybreak Imagery. 51 (left), W. Griffin. 51 (right), Perry
Slocum.
Perching Birds: 52 (art upper), Warren Cutler. 52 (art lower), Robert Cremins. 52, Ken Cole. 53
(upper), Marcia W. Griffen. 53 (lower) V.J. Anderson. 54 (art), Robert Cremins. 54 E.R. Degginger.
(art), Warren Cutler. 55 (left), Marcia W. Griffen. 55 (right), Alan G. Nelson.
Back Matter: 56 (art both), Robert Cremins. 56 John Gerlach. 57 (art both), Warren Cutler. 57 J.H.
Robinson. 60 Michael Fogden.

COVER: Its parents protect a four-month-old emperor penguin chick
through the harsh Antarctic winter. Emperors, which reach four feet in
height, are the largest of 17 species of penguins.

Composition for this book by the National Geographic Society Book Division. Printed and bound b
R.R. Donnelly & Sons Company, Willard, Ohio. Color separations by Graphic Art Services, Nashvil
Tennessee. Case cover printed by Inland Press, Menomonee Falls, Wisconsin.

Library of Congress CIP Data
Kostyal, K.M., 1951-
    Birds / by K.M. Kostyal.
      p.   cm — (National Geographic nature library)
    Includes index.
    Summary: Discusses the physical characteristics of birds and examines different kinds, including birds of prey,
wading birds, and flightless birds.
    ISBN 0-7922-7041-X
    1. Birds—Juvenile literature.   [1. Birds.]   I. Title.
  II. Series.
QL676.2.K67   1997
598—dc21   97-14562
                                                                                 CIP
                                                                                           A